Creative Milkshake Recip

Kids and Adults Alike

From Simple to Spectacular: Creating Sweet Masterpieces with Your

Blender & Ice Cream

The Ultimate Trilogy of Milkshake Madness!

By: Samantha Rich

home cooking

License Notes

Table of Contents

Introduction 6

1. White chocolate Milkshake 8

2. Blueberry Milkshake 10

3. Unicorn Milkshake 12

4. Strawberry Milkshake 15

5. Frosty Creamy Milkshake 17

6. Kiwi Strawberry Milkshake 19

7. Watermelon Milkshake 21

8. Berry Milkshake 23

9. Pineapple Milkshake with Coconut 25

10. Pineapple Cream Milkshake 27

11. Easy Cherry Milkshake 29

12. Cream Banana Pie Milkshake 31

13. Peach Milkshake 33

14. Lemon Milkshake 35

15. Caramel Banana Milkshake 37

16. Cherry Milkshake 39

17. Pumpkin Milkshake 41

18. Mango Milkshake 43

19. Dates Milkshake 45

20. Super Mango Milkshake 47

21. Apple Caramel Milkshake 49

22. Orange Milkshake 51

23. Apple Milkshake Without Ice Cream 53

24. Basic Berry Milkshake 55

25. Papaya Milkshake 57

26. Basic Vanilla Milkshake 59

27. Avocado Milkshake 61

28. Cheesecake milkshake 63

29. Funfetti Milkshake 65

30. Cream Peach Milkshake 67

31. Mango Milkshake Without Ice Cream 69

32. Cookie Cream Milkshake 71

33. Mocha Milkshake 73

34. Berry and Oat Milkshake 75

35. Strawberry Milkshake 77

36. Biscuit Creamy Milkshake 79

37. Oreo Milkshake 81

38. Minty Chocolate Milkshake 83

39. Cookie Dough Creamy Milkshake 85

40. Strong Flavored Chocolate Milkshake 87

41. Chocolate Cake Milkshake 89

42. Samoa Milkshake 91

43. Coconut Chocolate Milkshake 93

44. Oreo Chocolate Milkshake 95

45. Chocolate Cookie Milkshake 97

46. Banana Chocolate Milkshake 99

47. Peanut Butter Oreo Milkshake 101

48. Chocolate Pie Milkshake 103

Biography 105

Afterword's 106

Introduction

Milkshakes are a unique beverage, and a lot of people really enjoy them. It's widely available at ice cream parlors, sit-down restaurants, and fast food joints. However, nothing beats a handmade version. Why? For the simple reason that you may decide what goes into its creation.

Whoever thought up this miraculous beverage should be rewarded. Or, when did it first appear? Everyone who, like me, is completely obsessed with milkshakes, please read this.

Milk drinks have existed for a while, but storing milk was a hassle before refrigeration was introduced. In order to prevent the milk from going bad, it was necessary to consume it quickly. Thus, syllabub and posset were the first well-known milk-based beverages. They were created at the very least in the 16th century. The phrase "milkshake" was originally published in the Atlanta Constitution on May 17, 1886. To be fair, the first milkshakes were just flavored milk, although a very sugary one.

We absolutely like the hundreds of milkshake recipes available nowadays. To be honest, it's not simple to decide which one you want to have next. Therefore, I decided to compile *"Creative Milkshake Recipes for Kids and Adults Alike"* for this very reason. I've compiled a list of my favorite milkshake recipes that are so delicious that even the most discerning palates will like them.

To save time and effort, I made sure the preparation was straightforward. I also made sure to supply a variety of flavors, some of which went sans ice cream. Thus, you can still whip up a milkshake even if you're missing some of the more "fundamental" components.

Get the milkshake adventure rolling right now!

HHHHHHHHHHHHHHHHHHHHHHHHHHHHHHHHHHHHHH

1. White chocolate Milkshake

Preparation Time: 5 min

Duration: 5 min

Serving Sizes: 4 small glasses

Ingredient List:

- 1 tablespoon of white, pink and red sprinkles
- ¼ cup of chocolate chips, white
- ¼ cup of half and half
- 1 ½ cups of ice cream, Vanilla
- 1 cup of strawberries, frozen

HHHHHHHHHHHHHHHHHHHHHHHHHHHHHHHHHHHH

Methods:

a) Add the strawberries to a blender and blend them for half a minute.

b) Add the ice cream and blend it for about 15 seconds more.

c) Add the half & half and blend it for 10 more seconds.

d) Add the chocolate chips and blend for about 10 to 15 seconds.

e) Transfer the white chocolate milkshake into glasses and top it with sprinkles.

2. Blueberry Milkshake

Preparation Time: 5 min

Duration: 5 min

Serving Sizes: ¾ cup

Ingredient List:

- 2 cups of ice cream, vanilla
- 2 cups of milk
- 2 cups of blueberries, frozen
- 1 tablespoon of honey

HHHHHHHHHHHHHHHHHHHHHHHHHHHHHHHHHHHHHHHHHH

Methods:

a) Combine all of the ingredients in a blender.

b) Blend until the mixture is creamy and smooth.

c) Serve the blueberry milkshake immediately and enjoy!

3. Unicorn Milkshake

Preparation Time: 10 min

Duration: 10 min

Serving Sizes: 2

Ingredient List:

- 10 oz. (5 scoops) of ice cream, coconut
- 1 cup of frozen or fresh strawberries
- ½ cup of creamer
- ½ cup of marshmallows, fruity, small
- ¼ cup of vanilla frosting
- ¼ cup of white chocolate, chopped
- ½ cup of sprinkles
- Wafer cookies
- Rock candy
- Lollipops
- Whipped cream

HHHHHHHHHHHHHHHHHHHHHHHHHHHHHHHHHHHHH

Methods:

a) Combine the chocolate, strawberries, and ice cream in a blender. Blend the ingredients until they are creamy and smooth.

b) Snip the marshmallows in halves. Now press them inside 2 glasses.

c) Spread a very thin layer of vanilla frosting on the top rim. Roll them in sprinkles.

d) Divide the blended milkshake into the cups and top with the whipped cream. Sprinkle it with sprinkles.

e) Now decorate as you wish with lollipops, rock candy, wafer cookies, etc. Add unicorn straws and serve.

f) Enjoy!

4. Strawberry Milkshake

Preparation Time: 5 min **Cook:** 10 **Total Time:** 15 min

Serving Sizes: 1

Ingredient List:

- 2 cups of vanilla ice cream
- ¼ cup of strawberry syrup
- 1 strawberry, garnish
- 2 tablespoons of sugar

For the syrup:

- 2 cups of strawberries, quartered
- 1 cup of sugar
- 1 cup of water

HHHHHHHHHHHHHHHHHHHHHHHHHHHHHHHHHHHHH

Methods:

a) For the syrup: In a saucepan, add the strawberries, sugar, and water and simmer for a period of 10 minutes. Strain the mixture and let it cool.

b) Add the strawberry syrup, milk, and ice cream in a blender. Blend until the mixture is smooth.

c) Pour the milkshake into a serving glass, top it with one strawberry, and enjoy!

5. Frosty Creamy Milkshake

Preparation Time: 5 min **Cook:** 15 min **Total Time:** 20 min

Serving Sizes: 2

Ingredient List:

- ¼ cup of milk
- 6 oz. of Greek yogurt, plain
- 1 pint of ice cream, vanilla
- 2 tablespoons of water
- 2 teaspoons of sugar
- ¼ cup of blackberries
- ¼ cup of blueberries
- ¼ cup of raspberries
- ½ cup of ice

HHHHHHHHHHHHHHHHHHHHHHHHHHHHHHHHHHHHH

Methods:

a) In a saucepan add the berries, water, and sugar. Simmer until the berries break down and the sugar has Remove the mixture from the heat and let it cool.

b) Blend the remaining ingredients in a blender and divide it into 2 glasses.

c) Spoon the berries on top and stir it

d) Serve the milkshake immediately.

6. Kiwi Strawberry Milkshake

Preparation Time: 5 min

Duration: 5 min

Serving Sizes: 4

Ingredient List:

- 2 cups of fresh strawberries, sliced
- 2 cups of kiwi, peeled and sliced
- 2 cups of milk
- 2 cups of vanilla ice cream

HHHHHHHHHHHHHHHHHHHHHHHHHHHHHHHHHHHHHH

Methods:

a) Place the ingredients in a blender.

b) Blend until they are smooth.

c) Serve the milkshake in serving glasses and enjoy!

7. Watermelon Milkshake

Preparation Time: 10 min

Duration: 10 min

Serving Sizes: 3

Ingredient List:

- 2 cups of cubed and seeded watermelon
- 5 scoops of ice cream, vanilla
- 1 cup of milk, chilled
- 3 tablespoons of sugar

HHHHHHHHHHHHHHHHHHHHHHHHHHHHHHHHHHHHHHH

Methods:

a) In a blender add 3 scoops of ice cream, milk, sugar, and watermelon.

b) Blend the ingredients for 1 – 2 minutes. Chill the milkshake before serving.

c) Pour the milkshake into glasses and serve them with ice cream scoops on top.

8. Berry Milkshake

Preparation Time: 10 min **Cook:** 15 min **Total Time:** 25 min

Serving Sizes: 2

Ingredient List:

- ¼ cup of blackberries
- ¼ cup of blueberries
- ¼ cup of raspberries
- 2 tablespoons of water
- 2 teaspoons of sugar
- 1 pint of ice cream, vanilla
- 6 oz. Greek yogurt, plain
- ¼ cup of milk

HHHHHHHHHHHHHHHHHHHHHHHHHHHHHHHHHHHHH

Methods:

a) In a saucepan add the water, sugar, and berries. Turn on the stove to medium heat and let it simmer until the berries break down and the sugar has dissolved. Set the mixture aside to cool.

b) In a blender add the milk, yogurt, and ice cream. Blend until it is s Divide this into two serving glasses.

c) Spoon the cooled berries on top of the milkshake and stir very gently.

d) Serve the berry milkshake immediately and enjoy!

9. Pineapple Milkshake with Coconut

Preparation Time: 5 min

Duration: 5 min

Serving Sizes: 2

Ingredient List:

- ½ cup of coconut, shredded
- 1 cup of coconut milk
- 1 ½ cups ice cream, vanilla
- 1 ½ cups of pineapple, fresh, chopped

HHHHHHHHHHHHHHHHHHHHHHHHHHHHHHHHHHHHHHH

Methods:

a) Add the ice cream and pineapple in a blender and blend.

b) Add the milk and shredded coconut and blend for a few seconds.

c) Serve the milkshake in tall and big glasses and enjoy!

10. Pineapple Cream Milkshake

Preparation Time: 10 min

Duration: 10 min

Serving Sizes: 4

Ingredient List:

- 2 teaspoon of orange zest
- ½ teaspoon of vanilla extract
- 2 tablespoons of orange juice, fresh
- 1 ½ cups of milk
- ¼ cup of pineapple, diced
- 4 cups of ice cream, vanilla
- Orange slices

HHHHHHHHHHHHHHHHHHHHHHHHHHHHHHHHHHHHHH

Methods:

a) Add all of the ingredients to a blender.

b) Blend until they are

c) Serve the milkshake in tall and large glasses.

d) Top them with orange slices and enjoy.

11. Easy Cherry Milkshake

Preparation Time: 5 min

Duration: 5 min

Serving Sizes: 2

Ingredient List:

- 10 – 12 cherries, maraschino
- ¼ cup of cherry juice, maraschino
- ¾ cup of milk
- 10 scoops of ice cream, vanilla
- Whipping cream
- Chocolate syrup for topping

HHHHHHHHHHHHHHHHHHHHHHHHHHHHHHHHHHHHH

Methods:

a) Chop the maraschino cherries and set aside ½ of the cherries for garnish. Set this aside.

b) In a blender add cherry juice, milk, and ice cream. Blend until smooth. Now add the cherries and blend.

c) Pour the milkshake into serving glasses and top them with chocolate syrup, preserved cherries, and whipped cream.

d) Serve and enjoy!

12. Cream Banana Pie Milkshake

Preparation Time: 5 min

Duration: 5 min

Serving Sizes: 2

Ingredient List:

- Whipped cream
- 5 Wafers, vanilla
- ½ cup of milk, or less, according to taste
- 4 scoops of ice – cream, vanilla

HHHHHHHHHHHHHHHHHHHHHHHHHHHHHHHHHHHHH

Methods:

a) Place the ice cream, wafers, banana, and milk in a blender and blend until the desired consistency has been reached. Adjust the milk depending on the thickness you like.

b) Transfer the milkshake to a serving glass.

c) Top it with wafers, banana slices, and whipped cream. Enjoy!

13. Peach Milkshake

Preparation Time: 5 min

Duration: 5 min

Serving Sizes: 2

Ingredient List:

- 4 ripe peaches, medium, the pits removed and stems
- 4 oz. of half and half
- 1 teaspoon of vanilla extract
- 6 tablespoons of sugar (or to taste)
- 1 quart of vanilla ice cream, the brand you love

HHHHHHHHHHHHHHHHHHHHHHHHHHHHHHHHHHHHH

Methods:

a) Place the peaches in a blender. Add the half and half, vanilla, and sugar. Blend until very smooth.

b) Combine 1 cup of peach mix with 2 cups of vanilla ice cream, softened.

c) Serve the milkshake and enjoy!

14. Lemon Milkshake

Preparation Time: 5 min

Duration: 5 min

Serving Sizes: 2

Ingredient List:

- 3 cups of ice cream, vanilla
- ½ cup of milk
- ½ lemon juice
- 1 – 3 tablespoons of iced tea powder

HHHHHHHHHHHHHHHHHHHHHHHHHHHHHHHHHHHHHHHH

Methods:

a) Add the powder, milk, and ice cream to a blender.

b) Add the lemon juice and blend until smooth.

c) Serve the milkshake in glasses and enjoy!

15. Caramel Banana Milkshake

Preparation Time: 5 min

Duration: 5 min

Serving Sizes: 2

Ingredient List:

Caramel:

- 1 cup of whipping cream
- 2 oz. of butter, cut into small cubes
- 1 cup of sugar

Milkshake:

- 2 cups of milk
- 4 scoops of vanilla ice cream, + for topping
- 2 Bananas
- 4 teaspoons of caramel + for topping

HHHHHHHHHHHHHHHHHHHHHHHHHHHHHHHHHHHHHH

Methods:

a) Make the caramel: In a saucepan add the sugar and heat it. Once melted, turn on the stove to low heat and add the whipping cream. Now stir and cook the mixture while stirring constantly on medium heat. Once it starts to bubble, turn off the heat and set it Let it cool.

b) Blend the bananas, ice cream, and milk.

c) In 2 serving glasses add 2 teaspoons of caramel to each glass. Pour the milkshake equally into the glasses and top them with some ice cream and homemade caramel.

d) Serve and enjoy!

16. Cherry Milkshake

Preparation Time: 5 min

Duration: 5 min

Serving Sizes: 2

Ingredient List:

- 1 cup of frozen, halved, and pitted Cherries
- 3 vanilla Ice cream scoops
- ¼ cup of chilled milk

HHHHHHHHHHHHHHHHHHHHHHHHHHHHHHHHHHHH

Methods:

a) Add all of the ingredients to a blender.

b) Blend until smooth.

c) Transfer the milkshake to serving glasses and enjoy!

17. Pumpkin Milkshake

Preparation Time: 10 min

Duration: 10 min

Serving Sizes: 2

Ingredient List:

- 2/3 cup of pumpkin puree
- 1 ¼ cups of milk
- 1 ½ tablespoons of spice, pumpkin pie
- 3 cups of ice cream, vanilla
- For the topping: cinnamon, whipped cream, and sprinkles

HHHHHHHHHHHHHHHHHHHHHHHHHHHHHHHHHHHHH

Methods:

a) Add the milk, pumpkin, spice, and ice cream to a blender.

b) Blend until very smooth.

c) Transfer the milkshake to glasses and top them with sprinkles, whipped cream, and cinnamon.

d) Serve and enjoy!

18. Mango Milkshake

Preparation Time: 5 min

Duration: 5 min

Serving Sizes: 3 - 4

Ingredient List:

- Honey to taste
- 2 – 3 cups of milk, chilled
- 2 – 3 scoops of ice cream, vanilla
- 2 Mangos, ripe, cut into small cubes
- Ice cubes

HHHHHHHHHHHHHHHHHHHHHHHHHHHHHHHHHHHHH

Methods:

a) First blend the ice cubes and only 1/ 2 cup of milk. Once smooth you can add the remaining ingredients.

b) Blend until very smooth.

c) Serve and enjoy!

19. Dates Milkshake

Preparation Time: 5 min

Duration: 5 min

Serving Sizes: 4

Ingredient List:

- 1 ½ tablespoons of cocoa powder
- ½ cup of ice cream, vanilla
- 1 Banana, sliced
- 1 teaspoon of vanilla extract
- ½ cup of ice cubes
- 2 ½ cups of milk
- 12 dates

HHHHHHHHHHHHHHHHHHHHHHHHHHHHHHHHHHHH

Methods:

a) Start by removing the seeds from the dates.

b) Now add all of the ingredients to a blender.

c) Blend until you get a creamy and smooth consistency.

d) Transfer the milkshake to serving glasses.

e) Serve immediately and enjoy!

20. Super Mango Milkshake

Preparation Time: 5 min

Duration: 5 min

Serving Sizes: 4

Ingredient List:

- 2 cups of milk
- 1/8 teaspoon of nutmeg, ground
- 1/8 teaspoon of cinnamon
- 1 tablespoon of sugar
- 1 vanilla ice cream scoop, (optional)
- 1 banana, cut into chunks
- ½ Mango, diced, seeded, and peeled

Methods:

a) In a blender add the banana, mango, and ice cream (if using). Sprinkle it with nutmeg, cinnamon, and sugar.

b) Pour the milk and blend the ingredients until smooth.

c) Pour the milkshake into serving glasses and serve.

21. Apple Caramel Milkshake

Preparation Time: 5 min

Duration: 5 min

Serving Sizes:

Ingredient List:

- For the topping, caramel sauce, and whipped cream
- Whipped cream
- ¼ cup of milk
- 11/4 cups of caramel sauce
- ½ teaspoon of cinnamon
- 1 cup of apple butter
- 2 cups of vanilla ice cream, French

HHHHHHHHHHHHHHHHHHHHHHHHHHHHHHHHHHHH

Methods:

a) Place all of the ingredients in a blender.

b) Blend until smooth.

c) Transfer the milkshake to glasses and top them with caramel sauce and whipped cream.

22. Orange Milkshake

Preparation Time: 10 min

Duration: 10 min

Serving Sizes: 1

Ingredient List:

- 1 Orange, ripe and well peeled
- ½ cup of milk
- 1 ½ cups of ice cubes
- 3 tablespoons of maple syrup
- 2 teaspoons of vanilla extract
- Orange extract (if you want an intense flavor)

HHHHHHHHHHHHHHHHHHHHHHHHHHHHHHHHHHHH

Methods:

a) Place the orange in a blender. Blend until smooth.

b) Now add the other ingredients and blend again.

c) Pour the milkshake into a glass and serve immediately.

23. Apple Milkshake Without Ice Cream

Preparation Time: 5 min

Duration: 5 min

Serving Sizes: 2

Ingredient List:

- 1 large apple
- 2 cups of milk
- 1 teaspoon of cinnamon
- 2 tablespoons of sugar
- 2 - 4 ice cubes
- 20 cashews or almonds

HHHHHHHHHHHHHHHHHHHHHHHHHHHHHHHHHHHHHH

Methods:

a) Peel and then core the apples. Then, chop them and add them to the blender.

b) Add half of the milk, sugar, and nuts. Blend until you get a smooth texture.

c) Now add the ice cubes and the remaining milk. Blend again.

d) Pour the milkshake into glasses. Sprinkle them with cinnamon and serve.

e) Enjoy!

24. Basic Berry Milkshake

Preparation Time: 5 min

Duration: 5 min

Serving Sizes: 2

Ingredient List:

- 1 cup of blackberries
- 6 – 8 ice cubes
- ¼ cup of sugar
- 1 cup of heavy cream
- 1 cup of milk

HHHHHHHHHHHHHHHHHHHHHHHHHHHHHHHHHHHHHHHHH

Methods:

a) Combine the ingredients in a blender.

b) Blend until smooth.

c) Pour the milkshake into glasses and serve.

25. Papaya Milkshake

Preparation Time: 10 min

Duration: 10 min

Serving Sizes: 4

Ingredient List:

- ½ cup of ice
- ½ teaspoons of cinnamon, ground
- 1 teaspoon of vanilla extract
- 4 tablespoons of sugar
- 12 oz. of evaporated milk, canned
- 3 cups of cubed fresh Papaya (peeled)

HHHHHHHHHHHHHHHHHHHHHHHHHHHHHHHHHHHHH

Methods:

a) Add all ingredients to a blender. Blend until smooth. Taste it and add more sugar if desired.

b) Pour the milkshake into glasses and serve.

c) Enjoy!

26. Basic Vanilla Milkshake

Preparation Time: 5 min

Duration: 5 min

Serving Sizes: 2

Ingredient List:

- 2 – 3 drops of vanilla extract
- 1/3 cup of sugar
- 2 cups of milk
- 12 - 15 ice cubes

HHHHHHHHHHHHHHHHHHHHHHHHHHHHHHHHHHHHHHH

Methods:

a) Add ingredients to a blender.

b) Blend until very smooth.

c) Pour the milkshake into glasses and serve.

27. Avocado Milkshake

Preparation Time: 10 min

Duration: 10 min

Serving Sizes: 2

Ingredient List:

- 1 Avocado, ripe, pitted, and peeled
- ½ cup of milk
- ½ can of evaporated milk
- Lemon zest
- Sugar
- Vanilla extract
- Cherries
- 2/3 cup of whipping cream

HHHHHHHHHHHHHHHHHHHHHHHHHHHHHHHHHHHHHH

Methods:

a) Whip the cream with sugar and vanilla. Fold in some lemon zest. Set aside in the refrigerator.

b) Blend the remaining ingredients until smooth.

c) Put the milkshake in the glasses and top them with the whipping cream. Place one cherry per glass and serve.

d) Enjoy!

28. Cheesecake milkshake

Preparation Time: 5 min

Duration: 5 min

Serving Sizes:2

Ingredient List:

- ½ cup of sugar
- ¼ cup of milk
- ¼ cup of sour cream
- 4 oz. of cream cheese
- ½ teaspoon of vanilla extract
- 2 teaspoons of lemon juice
- Ice cubes
- For garnish: whipped cream and graham crackers

HHHHHHHHHHHHHHHHHHHHHHHHHHHHHHHHHHHHH

Methods:

a) Place the ingredients in a blender (except the garnishes).

b) Add ice as you blend to get the constancy you like.

c) Pour the milkshake into serving glasses and top them with whopped and one graham cracker per glass.

29. Funfetti Milkshake

Preparation Time: 5 min

Duration: 5 min

Serving Sizes: 1

Ingredient List:

- 3 tablespoons of cake mix, funfetti
- 1 cup of crushed ice
- ½ cup of vanilla yogurt, frozen
- ½ cup of skim milk

HHHHHHHHHHHHHHHHHHHHHHHHHHHHHHHHHHHHHHHH

Methods:

a) Blend the ingredients in a blender. Blend until smooth.

b) Dip the glass in sprinkles (optional).

c) Pour the milkshake into a glass and serve.

d) Enjoy!

30. Cream Peach Milkshake

Preparation Time: 15 min

Duration: 15 min

Serving Sizes: 2

Ingredient List:

- 1 cup of coconut milk
- 1 cup of peaches, frozen
- 2 pitted dates
- 2 tablespoons of hemp seeds
- 1 can of coconut milk
- ½ teaspoon of vanilla extract
- 2 – 3 tablespoons of maple syrup or to taste
- A drop of vanilla extract

HHHHHHHHHHHHHHHHHHHHHHHHHHHHHHHHHHHHHH

Methods:

a) First place the can of coconut milk in a refrigerator overnight or for a few hours. Once chilled well, scoop out only the creamy part. Add it to a bowl and add 1 tablespoon sweetener of choice. Add a drop of vanilla extract. Blend with a hand-held mixer until fluffy.

b) Now, place the remaining ingredients in a blender

c) Blend until smooth.

d) Pour the milkshake into serving glasses and top them with the coconut whipped cream. Serve.

31. Mango Milkshake Without Ice Cream

Preparation Time: 5 min

Duration: 5 min

Serving Sizes: 2

Ingredient List:

- 2 cups of chopped mango
- 2 cups of milk, frozen and crushed
- ½ cup of canned evaporated milk
- 2 tablespoons of sugar
- For garnish, mango pieces

HHHHHHHHHHHHHHHHHHHHHHHHHHHHHHHHHHHHHH

Methods:

a) Combine the ingredients in a blender.

b) Blend until smooth.

c) Pour the milkshake into glasses and top with mango pieces.

d) Serve and enjoy!

32. Cookie Cream Milkshake

Preparation Time: 5 min

Duration: 5 min

Serving Sizes:2

Ingredient List:

- 1 cup of evaporated milk
- ½ cup of cookies, chocolates, crushed
- ½ cup of gummy worms, sour
- 2/3 cup of chocolate milk

HHHHHHHHHHHHHHHHHHHHHHHHHHHHHHHHHHHHHH

Methods:

a) Place the ingredients in a blender (except for the gummies and 1 tablespoon of crushed cookies)

b) Blend until very smooth.

c) Pour the milkshake into two serving glasses and top with gummy worms and crushed cookies.

d) Serve and enjoy!

33. Mocha Milkshake

Preparation Time: 5 min

Duration: 5 min

Serving Sizes: 2

Ingredient List:

- 3 cups of milk, chilled
- 1 tablespoon of coffee powder, instant
- 2 teaspoons of unsweetened cocoa powder
- 1 cup of ice cubes
- 4 tablespoons of sugar
- For garnish: chocolate, grated

Methods:

a) In a blender add the cocoa powder, coffee powder, sugar, milk, and ice cubes.

b) Blend for about 3 minutes.

c) Pour the milkshake into glasses.

d) Sprinkle the top with chocolate and serve.

34. Berry and Oat Milkshake

Preparation Time: 5 min **Cook:** 5 min **Total Time:** 10 min

Serving Sizes: 1

Ingredient List:

- 1 cup of milk
- ½ cup of berries, mixed
- 1 cup of ice cubes
- 1/3 cup of porridge oats

HHHHHHHHHHHHHHHHHHHHHHHHHHHHHHHHHHHHHHH

Methods:

a) First, toast the oats in a pan for about 3 to 5 minutes.

b) Add them to a blender and add the remaining ingredients.

c) Blend until smooth.

d) Serve cold and enjoy it!

35. Strawberry Milkshake

Preparation Time: 5 min

Duration: 5 min

Serving Sizes: 2

Ingredient List:

- ½ cup of cream or milk
- 1 tablespoon of sugar
- ¼ teaspoon of vanilla
- ½ cup of strawberries, frozen
- Ice cubes
- Whipped Cream

HHHHHHHHHHHHHHHHHHHHHHHHHHHHHHHHHHHHHH

Methods:

a) Place all of the ingredients in a blender (except for the whipped cream).

b) Blend until smooth.

c) Transfer the milkshake into jars or serving glasses and top them with whipped cream.

d) Serve and enjoy!

36. Biscuit Creamy Milkshake

Preparation Time: 5 min

Duration: 5 min

Serving Sizes: 1

Ingredient List:

- 6 cream biscuits, vanilla
- 1 Banana
- 1 cup of milk
- ½ cup of oats
- For garnish: chocolate sprinkles and whipped cream

HHHHHHHHHHHHHHHHHHHHHHHHHHHHHHHHHHHHHHH

Methods:

a) Add the ingredients to a blender (except for the garnishes).

b) Blend until very smooth.

c) Pour the milkshake into a serving glass.

d) Top it with whipped cream and sprinkle with chocolate sprinkles.

e) Enjoy!

37. Oreo Milkshake

Preparation Time: 5min

Duration: 5 min

Serving Sizes: 1

Ingredient List:

- 4 oreo cookies
- 1 cup of milk, chilled
- ½ teaspoon of vanilla extract
- Ice cubes
- ½ tablespoon of sugar
- 1 tablespoon of chocolate syrup

HHHHHHHHHHHHHHHHHHHHHHHHHHHHHHHHHHHHHH

Methods:

a) Place all of the ingredients in a blender.

b) Blend for about a minute, until frothy and thick.

c) Pour the milkshake into a glass.

d) Garnish with oreo and serve.

38. Minty Chocolate Milkshake

Preparation Time: 5 min

Duration: 5 min

Serving Sizes: 2

Ingredient List:

- 2 cups of ice cream, vanilla
- ½ cup of milk
- 2 tablespoons of int, fresh or 2 teaspoons of peppermint flavor
- 1 drop of green color for food
- 2 tablespoons of chocolate chips
- Whipped cream

HHHHHHHHHHHHHHHHHHHHHHHHHHHHHHHHHHHHHH

Methods:

a) Place all of the ingredients in a blender except the whipped cream and chocolate chips.

b) Blend until smooth.

c) Transfer the milkshake to glasses and top them with whipped cream and chocolate chips.

d) Enjoy!

39. Cookie Dough Creamy Milkshake

Preparation Time: 5 min

Duration: 5 min

Serving Sizes: 4

Ingredient List:

- 2 cups of whipped cream
- 1 cup of chocolate syrup
- 1 ¼ cups of chocolate milk
- 5 scoops of ice cream, cookie dough
- Cherries (for garnish, optional)
- Ice cubes

HHHHHHHHHHHHHHHHHHHHHHHHHHHHHHHHHHHHHHH

Methods:

a) Add the ice cubes and ice cream to the blender.

b) Add 1 ¼ cup chocolate milk. Blend until smooth.

c) Add the syrup to the serving glasses.

d) Pour the milkshake in.

e) Top it with whipped cream and one cherry per each glass.

f) Serve and enjoy!

40. Strong Flavored Chocolate Milkshake

Preparation Time: 10 min

Duration: 10 min

Serving Sizes: 2

Ingredient List:

- 2 tablespoons of heavy cream
- 2 oz. of chopped German chocolate
- 1/3 cup of pecan coconut frosting, canned
- ¾ cup of milk
- 3 cups of ice cream, chocolate
- Toasted pecans and coconut for topping

HHHHHHHHHHHHHHHHHHHHHHHHHHHHHHHHHHHHH

Methods:

a) In a blender add the frosting, milk, and ice cream. Blend until smooth and pour into glasses.

b) Microwave the chocolate until melted.

c) Top the milkshakes with whipped cream, pecans, coconut, and melted chocolate.

d) Serve and enjoy!

41. Chocolate Cake Milkshake

Preparation Time: 5 min

Duration: 5 min

Serving Sizes: 4

Ingredient List:

- 1 cup of coconut, toasted, shredded (sweetened)
- ½ cup of milk
- ¼ cup of coconut cream
- 1 chocolate cake, slice
- 2 cups of ice cream, chocolate
- 2 cups of ice cream, vanilla

HHHHHHHHHHHHHHHHHHHHHHHHHHHHHHHHHHHHH

Methods:

a) In a blender add the ice cream, coconut cream, chocolate cake, and milk.

b) Blend until smooth.

c) Now add the toasted coconut and blend for a few seconds.

d) Transfer the milkshake to glasses and serve.

42. Samoa Milkshake

Preparation Time: 10 min **Cook:** 5 min **Total Time:** 15 min

Serving Sizes: 2

Ingredient List:

- Caramel Sauce
- Chocolate fudge sauce
- ½ cup of coconut, toasted
- ¾ cup of milk
- 4 scoops of vanilla Ice cream
- 5 – 6 Samoa cookies

HHHHHHHHHHHHHHHHHHHHHHHHHHHHHHHHHHHHHHH

Methods:

a) Toast the coconut over low.

b) Dip the glass in chocolate sauce and then in the coconut. Place in the freezer and let it set.

c) In a blender combine ¼ cup toasted coconut, milk, ice cream, and Samoa cookies. Blend until very smooth.

d) Take the glass from the freezer and add caramel and chocolate sauce inside the glass. Fill it up with the milkshake.

e) Top them with chocolate and caramel sauce and toasted coconut.

f) Enjoy!

43. Coconut Chocolate Milkshake

Preparation Time: 10 min

Duration: 10 min

Serving Sizes: 1

Ingredient List:

- 2 tablespoons of chocolate powder
- 3 scoops of ice cream, coconut
- 8 oz. of milk
- ¼ cup of coconut flakes, toasted
- ¼ cup of chocolate chips, semi-sweet

HHHHHHHHHHHHHHHHHHHHHHHHHHHHHHHHHHHHHH

Methods:

a) Melt the chocolate chips for 15 seconds in the microwave. Stir and melt again if needed. Dip the rim of the glass in the chocolate and then dunk it into the coconut. Set aside.

b) Now in a blender add the chocolate powder, ice cream, and milk. Plus, until smooth.

c) Pour the milkshake into the glasses and sprinkle with coconut and serve.

44. Oreo Chocolate Milkshake

Preparation Time: 10 min

Duration: 10 min

Serving Sizes: 1

Ingredient List:

- 5 tablespoons of ice cream, vanilla
- 2 cups of milk
- 7 - 9 oreo cookies
- 2 tablespoons of coconut flakes
- 1 Strawberry
- 10 ice cubes
- ½ cup of melted white chocolate

HHHHHHHHHHHHHHHHHHHHHHHHHHHHHHHHHHHHHH

Methods:

a) Combine all of the ingredients in a blender, except for the strawberries.

b) Blend until very smooth.

c) Pour the milkshake into a glass and top it with 1 strawberry and crushed Oreo cookie.

d) Enjoy!

45. Chocolate Cookie Milkshake

Preparation Time: 5 min

Duration: 5 min

Serving Sizes: 4

Ingredient List:

- 3 tablespoons of milk
- 4 scoops of ice cream, Vanilla
- 3 cookies, chocolate chip
- Whipped cream
- Cherry
- Caramel Sauce

HHHHHHHHHHHHHHHHHHHHHHHHHHHHHHHHHHHHH

Methods:

a) In a blender place the milk, ice cream, and cookies. Blend until smooth.

b) Transfer the milkshake to glasses and drizzle them with caramel sauce, top with whipped cream, cherry, and again with caramel sauce.

c) Serve and enjoy!

46. Banana Chocolate Milkshake

Preparation Time: 5 min

Duration: 5 min

Serving Sizes: 4

Ingredient List:

- 1 banana, frozen
- 5 scoops of Ice cream, vanilla
- ½ cup of milk
- ¼ cup of chocolate sauce
- 1/3 cup of peanut butter, creamy
- For garnish: chocolate sauce, cookies (crumbled), and peanut butter

HHHHHHHHHHHHHHHHHHHHHHHHHHHHHHHHHHHHHH

Methods:

a) Place all of the ingredients in a blender (except the garnishes).

b) Blend until smooth.

c) Top the milkshake with the garnishes and serve.

d) Enjoy!

47. Peanut Butter Oreo Milkshake

Preparation Time: 5 min

Duration: 5 min

Serving Sizes: 4

Ingredient List:

- 4 strawberries
- 1 teaspoon of vanilla
- 8 Oreo cookies
- 1/3 cup of peanut butter
- 3 cups of chocolate ice cream
- 1 cup of milk

HHHHHHHHHHHHHHHHHHHHHHHHHHHHHHHHHHHH

Methods:

a) Combine the ingredients in a blender.

b) Blend until smooth. Transfer the milkshake to serving glasses and top them with a strawberry.

c) Serve immediately and enjoy it.

48. Chocolate Pie Milkshake

Preparation Time: 5 min

Duration: 5 min

Serving Sizes: 4

Ingredient List:

- 1 – 2 slices of chocolate crème pie, store-bought
- 1 quart of ice cream, vanilla
- 2 teaspoons of honey or simple syrup
- ½ cup of milk
- Cherries
- Crackers
- Chocolate Sauce
- Whipping cream

HHHHHHHHHHHHHHHHHHHHHHHHHHHHHHHHHHHHHH

Methods:

a) Place the pie, ice cream, 2 tablespoons of syrup, and ¼ cup of milk in milk. Blend until very smooth.

b) Pour the milkshake into glasses.

c) Serve them with cracker crumbs, cheery, and chocolate sauce. Enjoy!

Biography

Samantha Rich is a dynamic and creative writer who has a passion for cooking and writing recipes. Born and raised in the United States, she has always had a love for food and the art of cooking. From a young age, Samantha was always eager to try new recipes and experiment with flavors, and her family encouraged her creativity in the kitchen.

Samantha's love for cooking and writing only grew as she got older, and she eventually pursued a degree in culinary arts and writing. She honed her skills in the kitchen, and her writing talent soon became apparent. She began publishing her recipes in local newspapers and food blogs, and her writing quickly caught the attention of others in the culinary world.

In her early twenties, Samantha decided to take her passion to the next level by writing a cookbook. Her first cookbook was a success, and she quickly gained Over the next few years, she continued to write more cookbooks, each one showcasing her unique voice and culinary creativity.

Today, Samantha Rich is a well-respected and beloved author in the cooking and writing community. Her cookbooks are enjoyed by home cooks and professional chefs alike, and she has become known for her ability to create recipes that are both delicious and accessible. Whether she's writing about classic comfort food or innovative new dishes, Samantha's writing is always infused with her love for cooking and her passion for sharing that love with others.

When she's not in the kitchen or writing, Samantha enjoys spending time with her family and friends, trying new restaurants, and exploring new recipes from around the world. She continues to be a sought-after speaker and presenter, and her fans are always eager to see what she'll come up with next.

Afterword's

Wow, what an incredible experience this has been. I couldn't have done it without your support and participation. As an author, I can only write the words, but it's up to the reader to bring them to life. And you did exactly that. You purchased this book, dedicated your time to reading it, and reached the end with me. I am deeply humbled.

While you've already done so much, I have one more request. I value feedback from my readers and would love to hear your thoughts on the book. I would be grateful if you could leave a review on Amazon. Not only will I see it, but it will also give others the opportunity to discover the book as well. The book community is a special one, and by sharing your thoughts, you are contributing to its growth and success.

Thank you for being so awesome.

Samantha Rich

Printed in Great Britain
by Amazon

35663329R00059